OPRAH WINFREY

Gloria D. Miklowitz

Dominie Press, Inc.

Publisher: Raymond Yuen
Editor: Bob Rowland
Designer: Greg DiGenti
Photo Credits: Steve Sands/New York
Newswire/Corbis (cover); Frank Trapper/Corbis
(Page 7); Brooks Kraft/Corbis (Page 18);
Mitchell Gerber/Corbis (Page 25); Douglas
Kirkland/Corbis (Page 31); and Corbis (Page 36)

Published by:

⚘ Dominie Press, Inc.

1949 Kellogg Avenue
Carlsbad, California 92008 USA

www.dominie.com

Paperback ISBN 0-7685-3045-8
Library Bound Edition ISBN 0-7685-3572-7
Printed in Singapore by PH Productions Pte Ltd
1 2 3 4 5 PH 07 06 05

Table of Contents

Chapter 1

Born into Poverty

What are the chances of a poor, African-American girl becoming a rich and famous woman in America?

Some would say the chances are virtually zero. But Oprah Winfrey stands to prove them wrong. Born to an impoverished, unmarried teenage mother in a small Mississippi town, Oprah today is an award-winning actress, a film and TV producer, and the host of a long-running and very popular talk show. *And* she is a multimillionaire.

How did she do it?

"I think of myself as somebody who from an early age knew I was responsible for myself and I *had* to make good," she told a reporter for *Ms. Magazine.* "The greatest contribution you can make to women's rights, to civil rights, is to be the absolute best at what you do."

Oprah Winfrey was born on November 29, 1954 in the small town of Koscuisko, Mississippi. She was named after a biblical character.

Oprah Winfrey poses with her award at the 30th annual People's Choice Awards ▶

Vernita Lee, her mother, was eighteen when Oprah was born. Her father, Vernon Winfrey, was under twenty-one and in the Army. They were not married.

The infant Oprah and her mother went to live with Vernita's mother, Hattie Mae Lee, on her tiny farm near Koscuisko. The small house had no running water, no electricity, and no indoor toilets. Oprah's grandparents raised pigs, chickens, and cows on the farm. "We grew everything we ate," Oprah said. "We sold eggs. It was very lonely out there in the country." The animals became her pets. She had only one good dress and one pair of shoes, and those were reserved for church each Sunday. Otherwise, she went barefoot.

When Oprah was four, her mother left to find work as a maid in Milwaukee,

Wisconsin, a thousand miles away. Grandma Hattie Mae became Oprah's mother and teacher. She expected Oprah, even at a very young age, to feed the chickens and pigs and carry water in a pail from the well to the house. Oprah attended church regularly and was taught to behave and be respectful to adults. When she misbehaved, she was struck with a small branch stripped of its leaves. Oprah had to select the branch. She was punished fairly often because she was curious, adventurous, and willful.

Oprah's grandmother loved her very much. At night she told her stories from the Bible and taught her to read. The two slept together in a feather bed and often sat and swung on the porch swing.

"I am what I am because of my grandmother," Oprah said. "My strength. My sense of reasoning. Everything." At the age of three, she was able to recite passages from the Bible at church. "The sisters sitting in the front row would fan themselves and nod to my grandmother," Oprah said. "They'd say, 'That child is gifted.'" She came to love performing for an audience. Wherever she went, she would ask people, "Do you want to hear me do something?"

When Oprah was five, she started kindergarten. She was bored because she already knew much of what was being taught. At one point, she wrote a note to her teacher. The note read, "Dear Miss New. I do not think I belong here." The teacher agreed, and Oprah was placed in first grade. A year later, she skipped over another grade.

Life changed for Oprah when she was six. Vernita decided she wanted Oprah to join her in Milwaukee. Oprah hated the big city. She thought it was dirty, noisy, and crowded. She missed her grandmother, the farm, and her pet animals. Her mother often worked long hours, and they were too poor to afford movies or other forms of entertainment. To amuse herself, Oprah caught cockroaches and made pets of them.

Vernita recognized that things weren't working out. After a year, she sent Oprah to live with Vernon, Oprah's father, who was now out of the Army and married.

How would Oprah, only seven years old, adjust to her new life?

Chapter 2

Life Offers a Fresh Start

Oprah's father lived in Nashville, Tennessee. He worked as a janitor, cleaning floors and at a hospital, scrubbing pots. He and his wife, Zelma, were strict parents. They set rules. Oprah had to make her bed each morning, wash dishes, and help with the cleaning.

All summer Zelma drilled Oprah on the multiplication tables that she had missed by skipping second grade. Her father gave her math problems to solve every day. "My stepmother was real tough," Oprah said. "I had to do book reports at home as well as at school, and so many vocabulary words."

Oprah blossomed under this kind of order and caring, and she did well in school. But when she returned to visit her mother the following summer, Vernita insisted that she stay with her. She expected to marry and move into a house so that her three children, including Oprah, could be together. Unfortunately, the marriage never took place.

Now, instead of a room to herself, Oprah shared a bedroom with a sister and brother in a small apartment. At school she did well, but she felt like an outsider. Being black in the North mattered much more than it did when she lived in the South. She kept to herself. People made fun of her because she was always sitting in a corner, reading. "My books were my only friends," she said.

Teachers had an important influence on Oprah's life. A fourth grade teacher recognized her intelligence and encouraged her. When she was thirteen, another teacher arranged for Oprah to get a scholarship to an excellent private school where she was the only black student. Even though she was liked and accepted there, she always felt poor and ugly. She envied the nice homes and lives her friends enjoyed.

At that point in her life, Oprah began to act out. When she needed glasses and her mother couldn't afford nice frames, she broke the frames so that she could get new ones. She ran away when she was fourteen. Then she became pregnant, but the baby died at birth. Vernita had had enough. She tried to have Oprah committed to a juvenile detention center. Oprah was shocked. She remembers wondering how all this could have happened to her.

When the detention center couldn't take Oprah because it was overcrowded, Vernita told her, "You've got to get out of my house, now." Then she phoned Vernon.

It was the best thing that could have happened to Oprah. Vernon and Zelma brought her back to Nashville. They were determined to straighten her out and give her a fresh start.

Chapter 3

Breaking into Broadcasting

"My father turned my life around by insisting that I be more than I was and by believing I could be more," Oprah told Alan Ebert in an interview for *Good Housekeeping* magazine. "His love of learning showed me the way," she said.

President George W. Bush talks with Oprah on "The Oprah Winfrey Show" during the presidential campaign of 2000

Vernon returned discipline to Oprah's life. When Oprah arrived in Nashville, she wore heavy makeup and skirts that were short and tight. She had forgotten the manners she'd been taught as a child. Vernon and Zelma wouldn't put up with that. Oprah not only had to do well in school, but she also had to work at Vernon's barbershop and grocery store and go to church regularly.

"Listen, girl," Vernon used to say. "If I tell you a mosquito can pull a wagon, don't ask me no questions. Just hitch him up!"

Oprah became president of her high school's student government and a member of the drama club. She was an exceptional debater and public speaker. When she was sixteen, she won a full scholarship to Tennessee State University. At seventeen, she took part in the White House Conference on Youth.

Not only was Oprah doing well at school, but she also discovered that she wasn't ugly, after all. At seventeen, she was 5 feet 6 inches tall and weighed 135 pounds. Just for fun, she decided to enter the Miss Fire Prevention Pageant in Nashville, although she had no hope of winning. She'd be the only young black woman in the pageant.

The judges asked each contestant what she hoped to do with her life. Some wanted to be teachers or to help in their family businesses. That morning, Oprah had seen Barbara Walters on the "Today" show. Why couldn't she be like her? "I want to be a journalist," she told the judges. Oprah's charm, beauty, and intelligence won over the judges. She became Nashville's first black Miss Fire Prevention.

Days after the pageant, Oprah went to pick up a watch that was part of her prize at a local radio station. There she met a disc jockey who was impressed by her voice and diction. "Why don't you try out for a job reading the news?" he suggested. Oprah thought he was joking, but when the station manager heard her, he offered her a job. At just seventeen years old, she began reading news after school every half hour until 8:30 at night. At first, she read the news without pay. But the station manager and others liked her so much, they paid her $100 a week. It was money that would be useful to cover college expenses.

Oprah was encouraged by the publicity she received as Miss Fire Prevention. Soon she decided to enter the Miss Nashville contest. And she won! Then she was a contestant in the Miss Black Tennessee contest. She won that, too! Her victories, she thinks now, were due to her poise and talent, rather than beauty. She could always answer the questions the judges asked, and she did well on the talent portion of the contests, usually by doing a dramatic reading.

When she was eighteen, Oprah left home for Hollywood, to compete in the Miss Black America Pageant. At some point, however, she lost interest in beauty contests. The fact that women are often judged mainly by their physical appearance made her uncomfortable. She decided to pursue a college education and a career in broadcasting.

Chapter 4

Finding What
She Could Do Best

Oprah was accepted at Tennessee State University, which was established in 1912 to serve African-American students. The school was only seven miles from her home, so she was able to continue reading the news at the radio station.

In 1971 the Civil Rights Movement was at its peak. "Everybody was angry for four years," Oprah said. "It was 'in' to be angry," and to protest the unfairness of treating people differently because of their race. But Oprah had no time to take an active part in the movement. She majored in speech and drama and had to be at the radio station every day after school. During that period in her life, she kept to herself and focused on her studies.

When Nashville TV station WTVF needed a co-anchor for the weekend six o'clock evening news, the station manager asked Oprah to interview for the job. She was a bright, talented African-American woman with a pleasant personality. People at the TV station knew that she would appeal to Nashville's large black population.

Oprah was still in college, but she was hired for the job. She was to become the first black newswoman the station had ever hired. They paid her $15,000 a year. Oprah worked with co-anchor Harry Chapman. Soon the program drew so much attention that they were promoted to do the news every weeknight.

In her last year at Tennessee University, with only a final project to complete, Oprah left to take a co-anchor job on WJZ-TV, in Baltimore, Maryland. Only twenty-two, she moved to a bigger city and had an apartment of her own. She appeared for the first time on the six o'clock news in Baltimore on August 16, 1976. But just seven months later, she lost the job. She wouldn't always read the words that were on the TelePrompTer, and she often showed emotion when she was on camera.

Oprah was still under contract with the station. She was assigned to co-host a new talk show called "People are Talking."

At last Oprah found what she could do best—just be herself. Her keen

Oprah Winfrey greets TV talk show host Barbara Walters at the 1995 Matrix Awards, sponsored by New York Women in Communications

insights, interesting questions, and humor attracted viewers. After the first show she thought, "Thank God, I've found what I was meant to do. It's like breathing to me."

It wasn't long before "People are Talking" drew more viewers in Baltimore than the very popular "Donahue" talk show, which aired at the same time from Chicago.

After six years in Baltimore, Oprah moved up again, this time to an even bigger city—Chicago—where she hosted her own half-hour talk show. On "A.M. Chicago," she interviewed top celebrities such as Tom Selleck, Shirley MacLaine and Stevie Wonder. And she explored issues she knew firsthand, such as overeating and child abuse.

The program took off! Before Oprah arrived, the show was ranked third in the Chicago area in viewer popularity. Four weeks after she took over, "A.M. Chicago" went to first place in its time slot, with the "Donahue" show in second place. Soon, Oprah's show was expanded to a full hour.

On her thirty-first birthday, Oprah appeared as a national celebrity on "The Tonight Show," with Johnny Carson as the host. Also on the show that night was Quincy Jones, a composer and record producer. A few months later Jones, who was traveling on business, turned on the TV in his hotel room and watched Oprah's program. He was working on a new movie about the suffering and triumphs of several African-American women based on the book *The Color Purple*, by Alice Walker. He wondered if Oprah might want to come to an audition to try out for a supporting role in the film.

"When I heard they were going to make a movie of it," Oprah said, "I thought, 'Oh, Lord, I will do anything to be involved—anything!' " Playing Sofia in that film took Oprah in an entirely new direction.

Chapter 5

Making a Difference

The film version of *The Color Purple* opened in December 1985. Reviewers praised Oprah's performance as Sofia, saying she was "shockingly good." And although she had only a supporting role, they said she was a "brazen delight." Vernon and Vernita went to see the film. It was the first movie they had seen in twenty-five years.

In addition to working on her talk show, Oprah continued to take acting roles. She played an important part in *Native Son* and starred in a TV miniseries called "The Women of Brewster Place," which depicted African-American women trying to survive in a poor, urban neighborhood. She also created a film company called Harpo Productions in order to gain control over her own time, her show, and her future career. (*Harpo* is *Oprah* spelled backwards.)

Oprah says she wants to "uplift people, encourage them, and give them a sense of hope about themselves." And she has been able to do just that, mainly through television.

Oprah Winfrey in the television miniseries
"The Women of Brewster Place"

Harpo Productions arranged for her talk show to be syndicated—or sold to TV stations all over the United States—with Oprah receiving part of the profits. The first syndicated show, called "The Oprah Winfrey Show," was televised in September 1986 to 138 cities. Her enthusiasm, honesty, humor, and down-to-earth manner delighted audiences. She came across as a regular person sharing problems her audience could relate to.

One project that was very important to Oprah was a film version of Toni Morrison's prize-winning novel, *Beloved*. The book deals with the plight of black people in the United States eight years after the Civil War. Oprah was advised that the film would appeal to a limited audience, but she fought to see it made because she believed that its message was important. Her role as Sethe in the film was highly praised because she brought the character to life. In preparing for each day's filming, Oprah said, "I kept slave documents in my trailer—slave ownership papers." And she would call aloud the names of those slaves before doing a scene.

By the end of the 1986 TV season, Oprah had earned $30 million, but she took only $1 million to spend. Ten years later she was considered the world's most highly paid entertainer, with an income of $171 million for 1995-96. In 1998 she was named one of the 100 most influential people of the twentieth century by *Time* magazine.

Money has made it possible for Oprah to "give back" to her family and friends, and to society. She bought a condominium in Milwaukee for her mother and gave her a monthly allowance so she wouldn't have to work. Vernon said he didn't need anything, but he accepted new tires for his truck and a bigger TV set for his barbershop. What he really wanted were tickets to the Mike Tyson-Tyrell Biggs boxing match in October 1987. Oprah got them for him, and later, she gave him a Mercedes-Benz.

*Oprah Winfrey appears with Willard Pugh
in the film adaptation of* **The Color Purple**

In 1987 Oprah returned to Tennessee
State University to finish her college
degree. She also donated $77,000 for
each of ten scholarships to the school
in Vernon's name. The scholarships
were based on student need and ability.
"The minute their grades drop," she
said, "they're out, because they have no

excuse." She continues to donate to the university to maintain the scholarships.

Working with former Illinois governor James Thompson, Oprah pushed for the passage of a bill through Congress that established national records of people convicted of offenses against children. That legislation, the National Child Protection Act of 1993, is known informally as the Oprah Bill.

She created Oprah's Book Club in 1996, devoting some of her television shows to discussing books and their authors with her audience. "I want books to become part of my audience's lifestyle," she said in an interview for *Publishers Weekly*.

Oprah has contributed generously to many social causes and has been involved with self-help projects working with families in poor neighborhoods.

She continues to seek ways to inspire people and give their lives meaning.

"I'm always looking for truth and its value in my life," she said in an interview that appeared in *Essence* magazine. "Material success is rewarding and a lot of fun, but it's not the most important thing in my life because I know when this is all over, the Master isn't going to ask me how many things I owned or how many television shows I did. I think the questions will be: What did I do to make a difference? Did I learn to live with love in my heart?"

Glossary

Audition – a test in the form of a short performance by an actor applying for a role in a movie or play.

Civil Rights Movement – a social struggle in the 1950s and '60s to oppose segregation and secure equal rights for black Americans.

Co-anchor – either of two TV journalists who report the news together on the same program.

Contestant – someone who takes part in an organized competition.

Contract – a legal agreement between two people or groups of people that explains what each person or group must do for the other.

Debating – talking about a subject at length in a formal exchange of opposing opinions.

Detention Center – a secure place where young people are kept, usually after they've been charged with committing a crime.

Diction – clarity of speech.

Disc Jockey – a person who plays recorded music on the radio or at a dance.

Discipline – order and control; enforcement of rules.

Envy – wanting somebody else's good fortune, success, or possessions.

Impoverished – very poor; destitute.

Influential – having the power to change something or have an effect on someone's opinion or behavior.

Juvenile – related to, or intended for, young people.

Keen – sharp; intense; fine-tuned; indicating an ability to grasp minor details.

Pageant – a large-scale show or production.

Plight – a very difficult or dangerous situation.

Poise – calm self-confidence, especially in tense situations.

Scholarship – financial aid given to a student by a college or university to help with living expenses, study, or travel.

TelePrompTer – a device that displays the words for someone to read on television, as in a newscast.

Time Slot – the regularly scheduled period when a TV or radio program is broadcast.

Willful – stubborn; obstinate; determined.